AF504473

Mommy and Daddy are Getting Divorced...

... now what?

Questions from Kids about the New Changes in Their Lives

By Ellen Ostroth and Nicole Delgado

Copyright © Ellen Ostroth and Nicole Delgado 2020

Technical design by Thane Ostroth

All Rights Reserved.
No parts of this book may be reproduced without permission and license.

JMND Press

Foreword

Mommy and Daddy are getting divorced. Andy, Mandy, and their dog Sandy have questions about the changes occurring in their lives.

One thing they learn is Mommy and Daddy's love for them is forever!

Acknowledgments

This book is for every child who ever got caught up in the confusion of divorce. It addresses some of the vital questions that children have but may be afraid to ask.

Families are always families, no matter what changes, no matter how they look, or how much time goes by. Love truly is forever!

Andy was very angry. His sister Mandy was very sad. Both felt a little bit afraid.

Mommy and Daddy were getting a divorce.

Andy and Mandy did not know what that would mean for them. They had always been a happy family in one house, hadn't they?

Now Mommy and Daddy would live apart and Andy and Mandy would now have two homes.

Mommy and Daddy said the divorce was not Andy or Mandy's fault. They said it was Mommy and Daddy's fault.

That's what they said, but Andy and Mandy weren't so sure.

Daddy was gone a lot and Mommy kept crying. Andy and Mandy wondered if Mommy blamed Daddy. Did Daddy blame Mommy?

Andy and Mandy just didn't know.

Their pet dog Sandy was glum. She knew things were changing, too.

Mandy was feeling shy. She had a really big question she needed to ask.

"Is the divorce my fault?" She said in a small voice. Mandy was blaming herself because she had been bad. She had not picked up her toys when Mommy told her to.

Andy grew quiet. He was afraid the divorce was his fault because he had not done all his homework. Even worse, he had lied about it when Daddy had asked him.

He was pretty sure Mommy and Daddy's divorce was his entire fault.

Both Andy and Mandy felt like crying.

"Oh, no. No, baby, no!" Mommy looks surprised. "A divorce is never the fault of the children."

"Absolutely not," said Daddy. "A divorce is between two parents but everyone is still a family."

Andy and Mandy were relieved. Even Sandy looked happier.

"You're not getting divorced because I was picking on Mandy and her friends, are you?" That was the other secret fear that Andy had kept inside himself.

"No, darling. Brothers and sisters have quarrels. Mommies and daddies know that from when they were small and lived with their brothers and sisters."

Andy felt a lot better

"Those brothers and sisters are now your uncles and aunts. They will always be your uncles and aunts, even after a divorce."

That made Mandy happier.

"Do you mean our cousins are still our cousins?"

"Yes. For always and always," Mommy said.

Andy and Mandy were relieved.

"Are Nana and Grandpa still our grandparents?" Mandy was anxious to know.

"Yes! They are your grandma and grandpa for ever and ever." Both Mommy and Daddy said it at the same time.

"If we're all still family, then why can't we keep living together in our house?" Andy and Mandy asked.

"It's because Mommy and Daddy are going to be doing different things and meeting new people. Won't that be fun?"

Sandy wagged her tail hopefully, but Andy and Mandy weren't so sure.

"Don't you and Mommy love each other anymore?" Andy asked.

"Yes, of course," Daddy said. "But in a different way now than we did before."

"Do you love us in a different way than before?" Mandy needed to know.

"Only to love you both more than ever, if such a thing was even possible!" Mommy hugged them both.

Sandy thumped her tail on the floor.

"Yes, we still love you, too." Daddy scratched Sandy behind the ears, just the way she liked it.

"This will be a new adventure for all of us!" Mommy tried to sound happy.

Daddy looked out the window. He seemed sad, too.

Andy and Mandy looked at each other. New adventures could be fun…

But Mandy was concerned. "Where will Sandy live?"

"She will live with all of us. When you are Mommy's house, she will be there. When you are at my house, she can come, too." Daddy was smiling again.

Andy, Mandy and Sandy all felt better.

"How come we have to change schools?" Mandy had just finished 1st grade. She had met her new best friend there.

Andy was going into fifth grade. It was his last year at the same school he had always gone to. Many of his friends lived in the neighborhood. Yet a new school and new friends was kind of exciting. Andy just wasn't sure how he felt.

"Sometimes in divorce, you get to stay in your same house or school. Sometimes both Mommy and Daddy need to get new houses." Daddy was trying to explain.

Mommy was busy trying not to cry.

"It's a double adventure to have two homes. Two new bedrooms. Lots of new friends. Won't a new school be a great, new adventure?" Daddy was trying to sound really happy.

Andy and Mandy nodded to make Mommy and Daddy feel better, but they just didn't know yet.

"But I'll miss my friends!" Mandy wailed. She couldn't help it. She started to cry.

Daddy put Mandy on his lap and hugged her tight.

"I promise it will be okay. You'll see." Mandy felt better.

Daddy always kept his word.

"You can invite your friends from your old school to spend the night in your new house. Won't that be fun?"

Mommy sniffled into a handkerchief but Andy thought she had a great idea. Sleepovers did sound like fun adventures!

Andy smiled. He could keep his friends, plus make new friends!

"I'll miss the park," Mandy cried.

"No, you won't," said Mommy, starting to sound happy again.
"We will have new parks and places to go. Plus, we can come back
and visit this park. We will even pack a picnic lunch!"

Mandy smiled. That did sound like fun!

"Can we still take swim lessons?" Andy wanted to know. He was becoming a very good swimmer.

"Of course! We want you to." Mommy looked even happier.

"My new house is an apartment. It has a swimming pool that everyone who lives there can use. It's an easy way to meet the other kids." Daddy was looking pretty excited, too

Andy and Mandy smiled at each other. A swimming pool would be fun!

Mommy said, "The new little house I have has a fenced yard for Sandy to play in. Plus, it has a swing set and slide for you kids."

Sandy barked and everyone laughed.

A swing set sounded like fun to Mandy. Andy was already planning to build a fort with his new friends.

"Will we still go to the movies and eat pizza sometimes?" Mandy was hopeful.

"Of course!" Both Mommy and Daddy said it at the same time. They looked at each other, and then laughed.

Andy and Mandy thought about it some more.

"But Daddy, I will miss you when I'm a Mommy's house." Mandy pouted.

"Mom, I'll miss you when we're with Dad." Andy was worried about his Mom being alone.

"We can all talk by telephone every day, if we want," Mommy reassured them.

"Video phone! We can see and hear each other all the time," Daddy said, holding up his cell phone.

"In fact, we have a surprise for each of you." Mommy seemed excited. She looked at Daddy, who smiled and left the room.

Then Daddy was right back, pulling two small rolling suitcases. One had footballs, soccer balls, baseballs and basketballs all over it.

"Neat!" Andy jumped up to take a look. He loved sports!

Mandy was excited by the other overnight bag. It was purple and pink with unicorns and rainbows. Her favorites!

"You will both have clothes and toothbrushes, books and games at each house. These you can use to bring whatever extra-special things you want, too." Daddy explained.

"Like my action figure toys and video games?" Andy was happy.

I can bring my favorite plushy toys and my special blanket?"
Mandy was relieved.

"What about Sandy?"

"I'm glad you asked," Mommy said.

She left the room and came back with a little rolling case that had kittens and puppies on it. When she opened it, there were chew bones, treat boxes, a squeaky toy and a leash for taking walks, all neatly packed inside.

"Arf!" Sandy jumped up and barked, tail wagging with joy.

The whole family laughed. Maybe divorce wasn't so scary after all.

"Every family is always a family. Families grow and change through marriage; divorce; even adding more children. It doesn't matter what colors, genders or religions families are. It doesn't matter how far apart people live or even if someone passes away. Your family is your family forever!"

The End.

Resources for Staying Connected...*at any age!*

Zoom/ Face Time etc	Set up regular visual call times
Marco Polo App	Video messaging
Texts and emojis	Send often
Phone call	Try to arrange a regular time
"Thinking of you" notes	In a lunchbox or backpack
Mail a funny card for each child	To the other parent's address
Have the children draw pictures	Frame them; display them
Private diary or journal writing	Respect your child's privacy
Small portable photo albums	Let children pick favorite pictures
Friendship lamp (www.friendshiplamp.com)	A quick, fun way to say "hello"
Messenger App	Quick family fun
Instagram & Facebook	Family photos
Family You Tube channel	Private family video postings

About the Authors

Nicole Delgado (AKA Danielle Real) is the author of <u>A Walking Disaster</u> <u>Mystery</u> series, Book I; "Last Name Unknown." Book II is in the works. Nicole has co-authored the successful "Oz will Fall" series with John Malone. Look for Book IV coming soon on Amazon. She has worked with and mentored autistic children, as well as being a Domestic Violence counselor.

Ellen Ostroth is a lawyer who has done free legal aid, pro bono and nonprofit, as well as Guardian ad litem work to protect children.

Ellen and Nicole, both having been divorced and both the children of divorced parents, decided with divorce so prevalent in our society, they would write a book to help children transition through the many changes.

Parents and kids can reach them at stonewisdom555@yahoo.com.

Read Ellen's other books: The "Moo to Poo" children's book for potty training. For adults, the <u>Elandra Spiritual Warrior Trilogy</u> <u>series</u>: The Art of Beauty; The Art of Betrayal; The Art of Being plus; The Art of Bravery, on Amazon.com. Her book "The How-To Shamanic Book for Laypeople" is co-authored with her husband, Thane.

Read Ellen's blog at www.stonewisdom.net. Nicole and Ellen will also be found on Instagram and Facebook.

Look for family-friendly *Divine Whisperings* on YouTube.com, promoting sleep and self-confidence.

www.ingramcontent.com/pod-product-compliance
Lightning Source LLC
Chambersburg PA
CBHW042120110726
48006CB00002B/706